Maths made Merry

Workbook Grade 2

Om KIDZ
An imprint of Om Books International

COUNTING ON THE CLOUDS

Help the aliens reach their spaceship. Fill up the empty clouds with the missing numbers.

101									191
	112								
						163			
105			135						
								186	
	117								
					158				
110		130			160			190	200

COMET RIDER

Help the little aliens write the names of the shapes that they found on our planet.

COMET CLASS

Help Casper the Comet write the number names next to the numbers.

101	
115	
120	
129	
133	
141	
148	
150	

DISCOVER SPACE

Count the objects and fill in the blanks correctly to help Argus the Astronaut learn about space.

I can see ________ space shuttles.

I can see ________ planets.

I can see ________ comets.

I can see ________ spaceships.

SHOOTING STARS

Solve the sums on the stars below.

9 – 3 = ___

31 – 9 = ___

20 – 8 = ___

15 – 7 = ___

39 – 4 = ___

19 – 9 = ___

26 – 10 = ___

42 – 16 = ___

AROUND THE WORLD

Drogo the Alien is trying to find the strongest asteroid of them all. Solve the sums on the asteroid and circle the one with the highest value to help him.

13 + 30 = ______

57 + 22 = ______

62 + 34 = ______

74 + 19 = ______

19 + 54 = ______

51 + 35 = ______

SKIPPING OVER SPACESHIPS

Help the aliens to skip and count their way to the spaceship!
Follow the instructions to skip and count.

Skip to the count of 2.

10,12 ___ ___ ___ ___ ___ ___.

Skip to the count of 10.

10 ___ ___ ___ ___ ___ ___ ___ ___ 100.

Skip to the count of 5.

20 ___ ___ ___ 40 ___ ___ ___.

OFF TO EARTH!

These aliens are trying to visit our planet. Read the distances on each planet and match the aliens to the correct ordinal numbers.

SPACE VALUES

Andy the Astronaut wants to travel to the Math Star, but he must crack the code first. Read the place value sentences and write the correct numbers to crack the code.

Six tens and five ones =

Three tens and seven ones =

One ten and three ones =

Nine tens and eight ones =

Four tens and one one =

Eight tens and two ones =

Five tens and three ones = ☐

Two tens and two ones = ☐

Seven tens and four ones = ☐

Nine tens and zero ones = ☐

Zero tens and nine ones = ☐

NUMBER SORTER

Sort the stars by connecting them to the correct basket.

VALUE WOES

Help these aliens understand the values of the objects below by placing <, > or = correctly in each set.

TANGLED TROUBLE

Untangle the ropes and match these sums to their values.

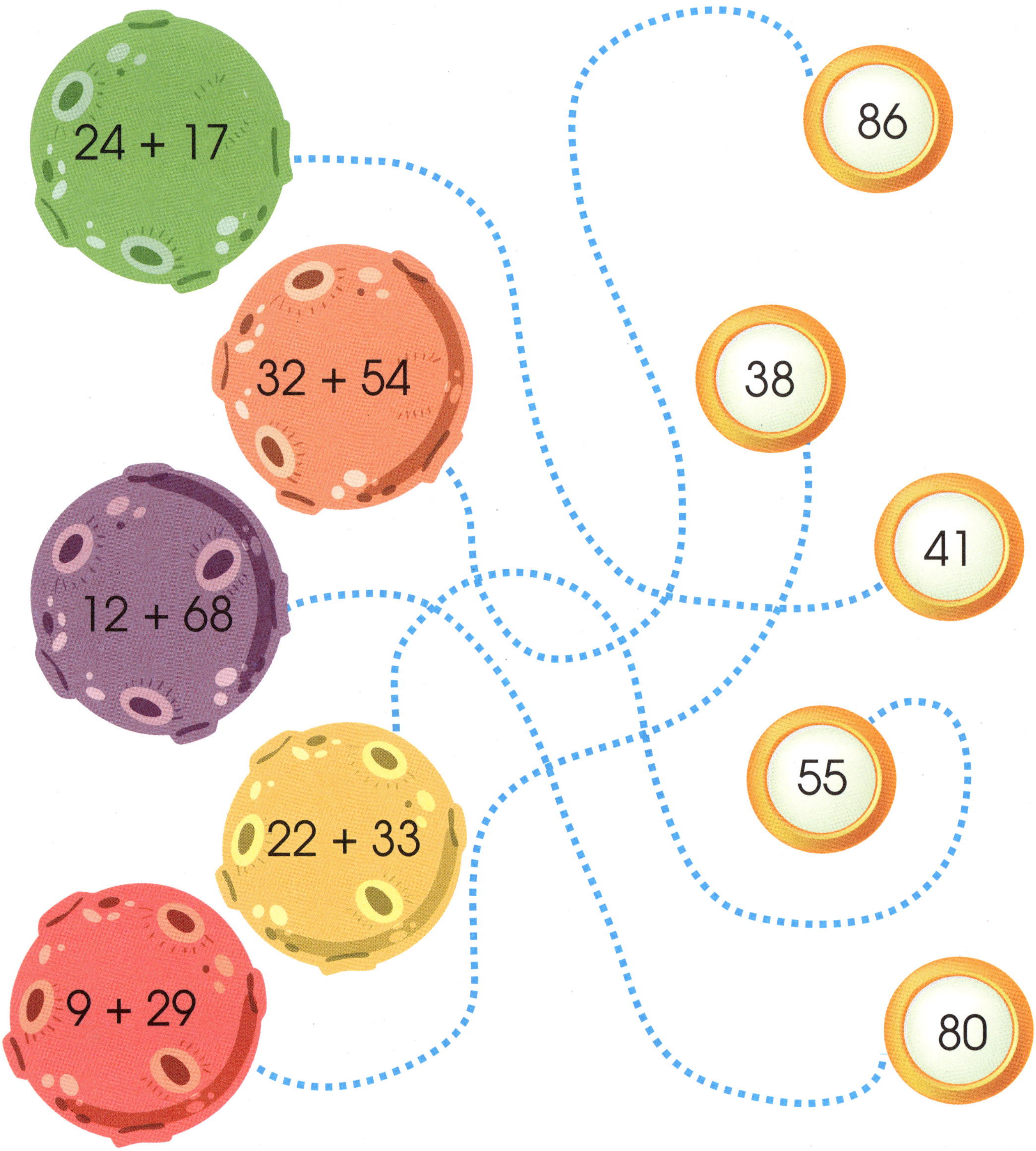

MOONY MEASURES

Number the objects on the moons from shortest to longest in each row.

BIG OR SMALL?

Circle the big spaceships and tick the small ones.

NEAR AND FAR

Number the planets according to their distance from the Sun, 1 being the nearest and 8 being the farthest.

FRACTION FUN

Help these aliens learn their fractions by colouring the correct number of parts below.

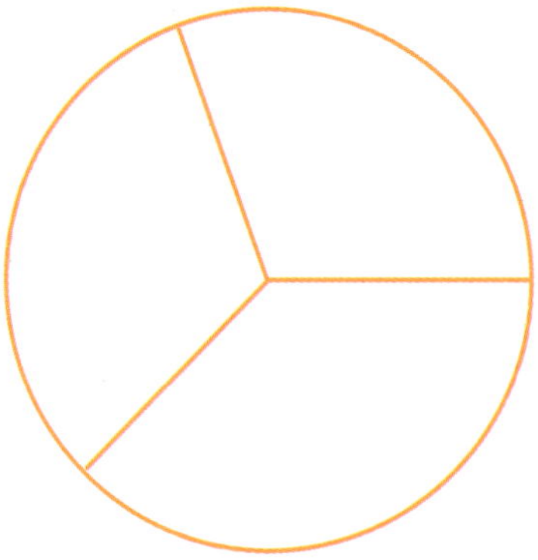

$\frac{1}{3}$

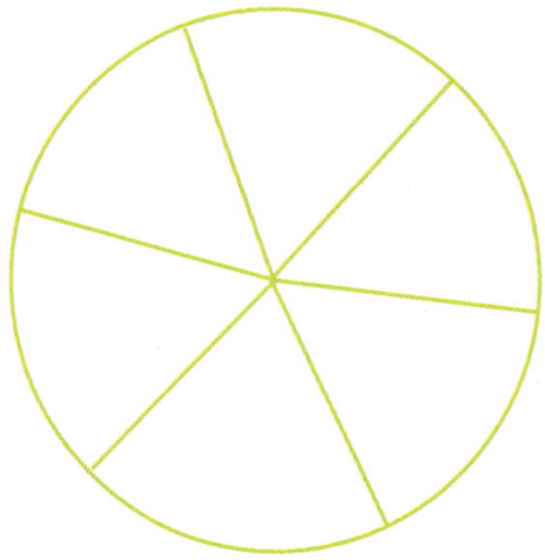

$\frac{4}{6}$

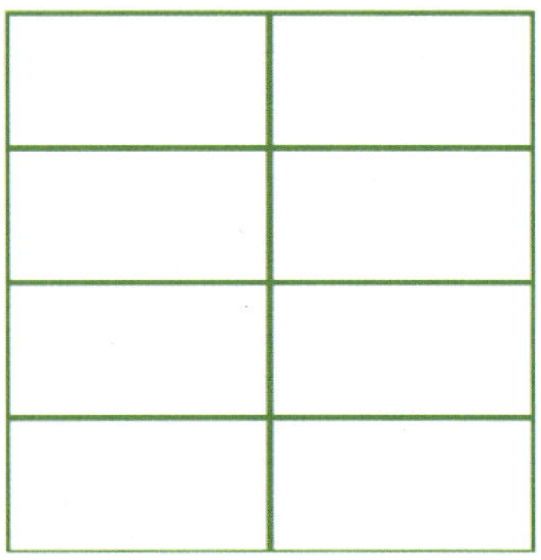

$\frac{4}{8}$

$\frac{2}{8}$

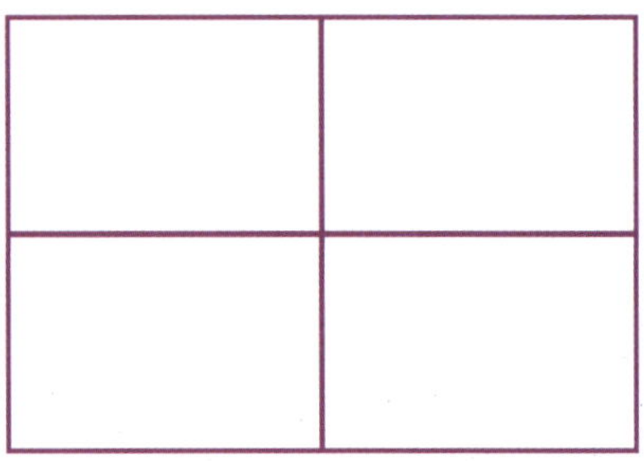

$\frac{1}{4}$

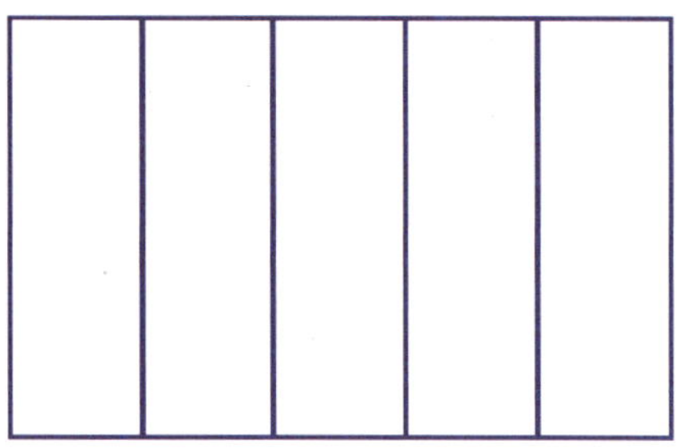

$\frac{4}{5}$

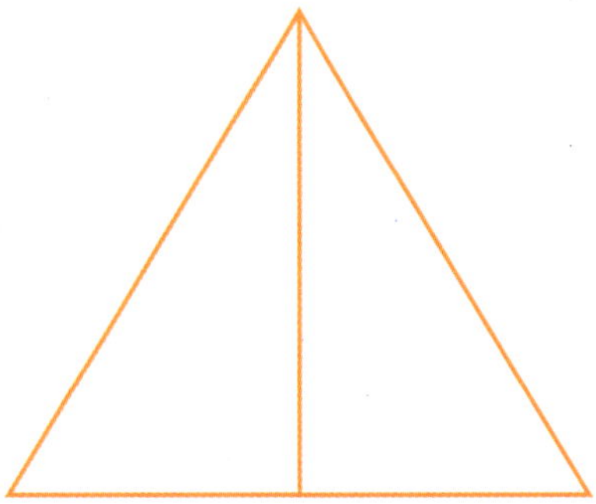

$\frac{1}{2}$

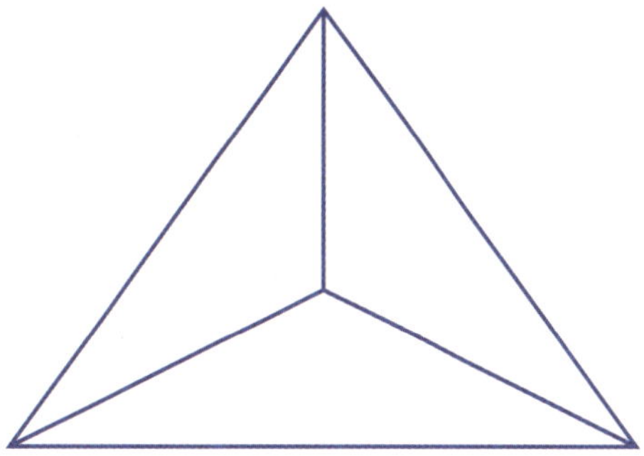

$\frac{2}{3}$

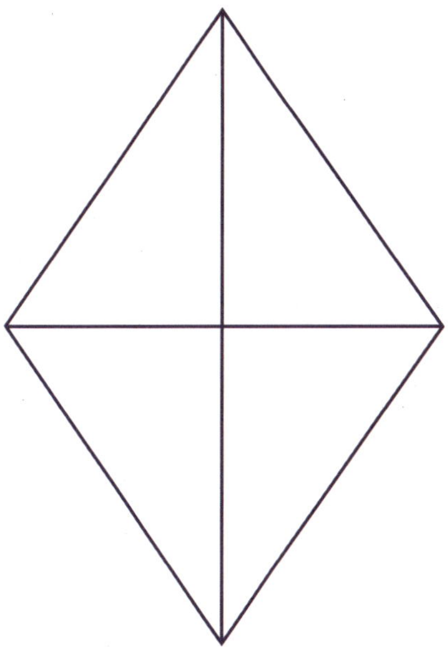

$\frac{4}{4}$

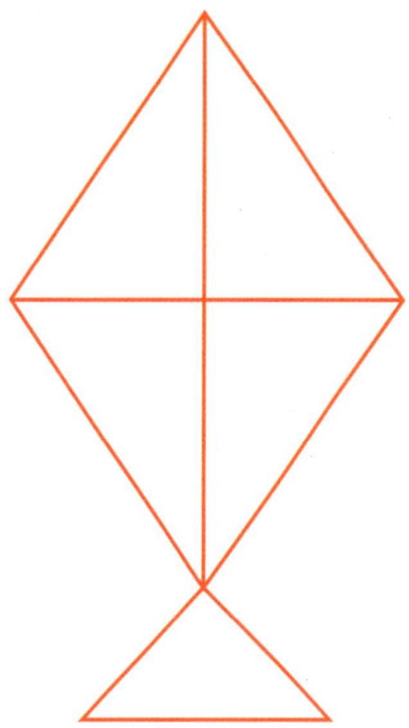

$\frac{1}{5}$

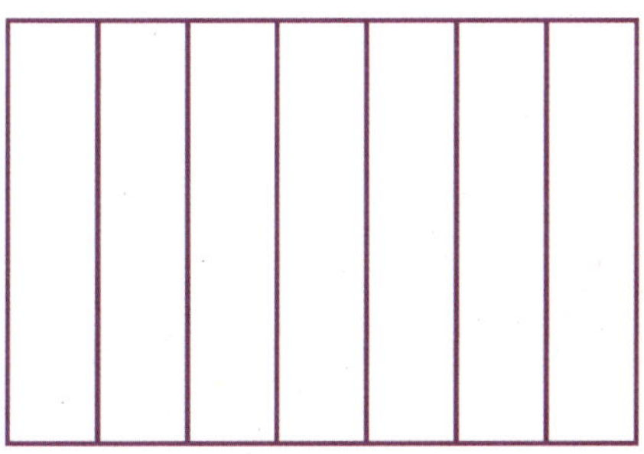

$\frac{2}{7}$

$\frac{7}{10}$

FRACTIONED FIGURES

Look at the spaceships, count the coloured ones and write their fractions alongside. One is done for you.

$\frac{3}{4}$

WEIGHTY WOES

Look at the aliens and tick the boxes under the heavier ones.

35 kg ☐

52 kg ☐

43 kg ☐

65 kg ☐

23 kg ☐

96 kg ☐

10 kg ☐

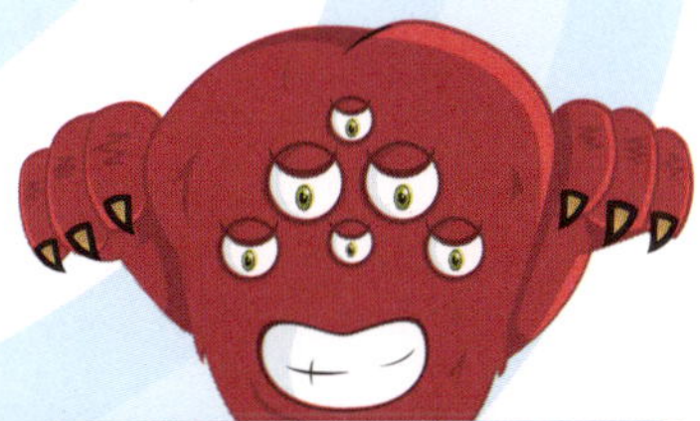

13 kg ☐

WORD WHIZ

Let's solve these word problems and reach the rocket!

Angus Astroboy has 15 rockets. Aliens Bados steals 3 of them. How many does he have left?

Alien Hypo buys 16 cups of coffee. Professor Curio gives him 24 cups more. How many does he have in all?

Alien Rumbly bought 24 peaches. He distributed 17. How many does he have now?

Argo Astroboy has 10 pens. Allie Astrogirl gave him 12 more. How many does he have now?

Allie Astrogirl bought 30 spacesuits.
She gave 15 of them to her friends.
How many does she have now?

20 comets were flying in the sky.
Alien Gobbleson ate 7 of them.
How many comets are left now?

31 stars were twinkling in the sky.
A giant cloud moved and showed
14 more. How many are twinkling now?

MONEY MAKERS

Help Addie the Alien count the notes and write their sums in the given box.

+

= ☐

+

= ☐

+

= ☐

+

= ☐

+

= ☐

CHANGE PLEASE!

These aliens have messed up their purchase amounts!
Count the coins and solve the sums to help them out.

+

= ☐

+

+

= ☐

+

= ☐

+

= ☐

EXPANDING GALAXIES

Expand the numbers on the galaxies below.
One is done for you.

110 = 100 + 10 + 0

95 =

115 =

78 =

58 =

135 =

120 =

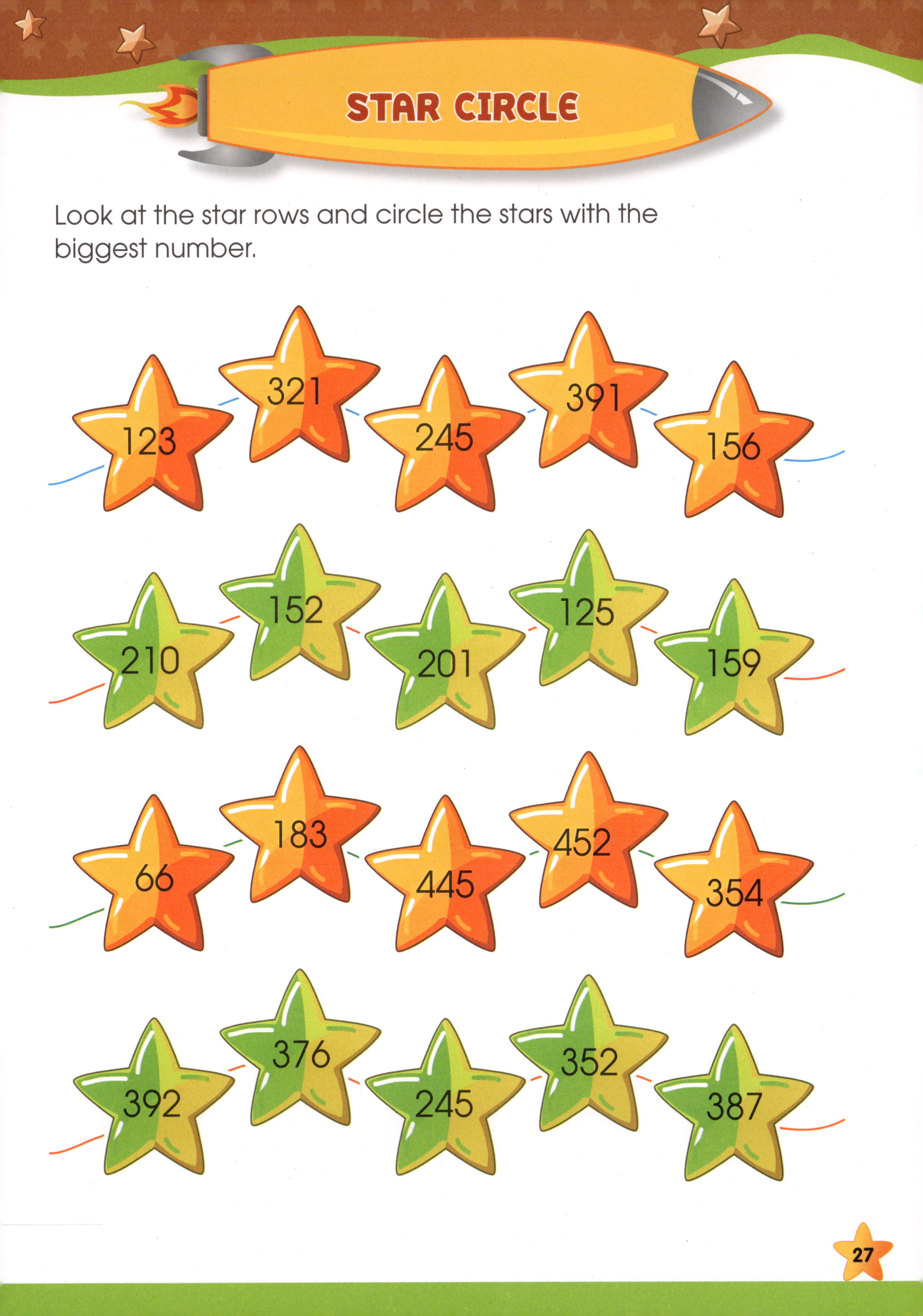

STAR CIRCLE

Look at the star rows and circle the stars with the biggest number.

123 321 245 391 156

210 152 201 125 159

66 183 445 452 354

392 376 245 352 387

ALIEN 'O CLOCK

These aliens bought some watches but don't know how to tell time. Can you read their watches and tell the time in them?

MULTI-TRAVELS

Help Argo the Astronaut travel to the right space station by following the path with multiples of 3.

MATH MAYHEM

Solve the sums on the stars below.

5 x 3 = ____

6 x 3 = ____

12 + 4 = ____

32 – 14 = ____

4 ÷ 2 = ____

29 + 20 = ____

16 – 10 = ____

9 ÷ 3 = ____

ANSWERS

Page 2

101	111	121	131	141	151	161	171	181	191
102	112	122	132	142	152	162	172	182	192
103	113	123	133	143	153	163	173	183	193
104	114	124	134	144	154	164	174	184	194
105	115	125	135	145	155	165	175	185	195
106	116	126	136	146	156	166	176	186	196
107	117	127	137	147	157	167	177	187	197
108	118	128	138	148	158	168	178	188	198
109	119	129	139	149	159	169	179	189	199
110	120	130	140	150	160	170	180	190	200

Enter

Page 3

Page 4

101	One hundred and one
115	One hundred and fifteen
120	One hundred and twenty
129	One hundred and twenty-nine
133	One hundred and thirty-three
141	One hundred and forty-one
148	One hundred and forty-eight
150	One hundred and fifty

Page 5

I can see 10 space shuttles.

I can see 8 planets.

I can see 9 comets.

I can see 7 spaceships.

Page 6

9 – 3 = 6

15 – 7 = 8

20 – 8 = 12

31 – 9 = 22

39 – 4 = 35

19 – 9 = 10

26 – 10 = 16

42 – 16 = 26

Page 7

13 + 30 = 43

57 + 22 = 79

74 + 19 = 93

62 + 34 = 96

19 + 54 = 73

51 + 35 = 86

Page 8

Skip to the count of 2.
10, 12 14 16 18 20 22 24.

Skip to the count of 10.
10 20 30 40 50 60 70 80 90 100.

Skip to the count of 5.
20 25 30 35 40 45 50 55.

Page 9

Page 10

Six tens and five ones	–	**65**
Three tens and seven ones	–	**37**
One ten and three ones	–	**13**
Nine tens and eight ones	–	**98**
Four tens and one one	–	**41**
Eight tens and two ones	–	**82**
Five tens and three ones	–	**53**
Two tens and two ones	–	**22**
Seven tens and four ones	–	**74**
Nine tens and zero ones	–	**90**
Zero tens and nine ones	–	**09**

Page 12

Page 13

Page 14

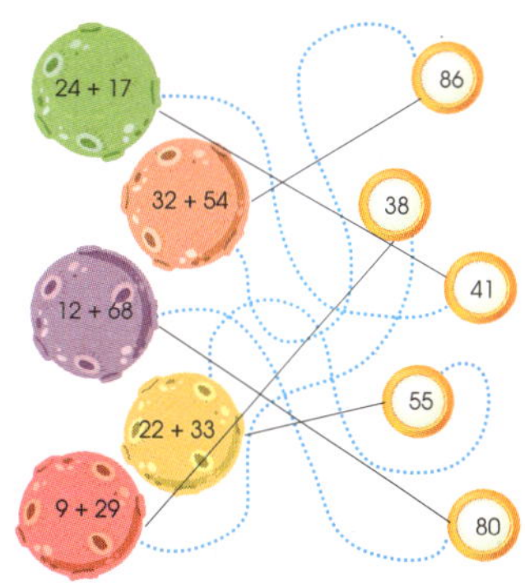

Page 15

Page 16

Page 17

Page 18

ANSWERS

Page 19

Page 20

Page 21

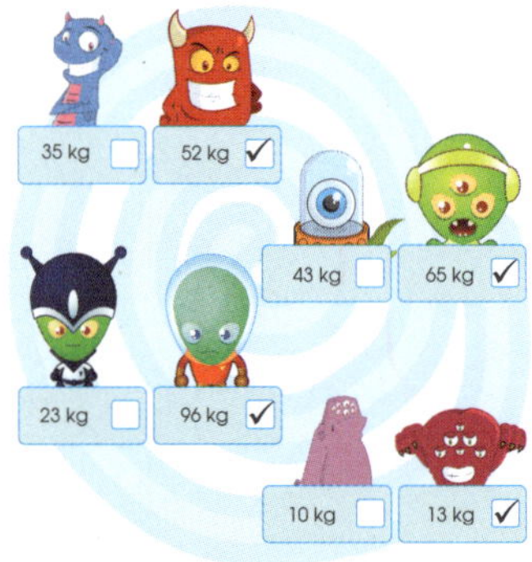

Page 22

Page 23

Page 24

Page 25

Page 26

110 = 100 + 10 + 0

95 = 90 + 5

78 = 70 + 8

115 = 100 + 10 + 5

58 = 50 + 8

120 = 100 + 20 + 0

135 = 100 + 30 + 5

Page 27

Page 28

Page 29

Page 30

6 x 3 = 18

5 x 3 = 15

12 + 4 = 16

4 + 2 = 2

32 – 14 = 18

29 + 20 = 49

16 – 10 = 6

9 + 3 = 3